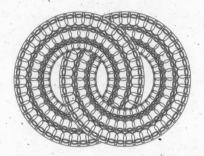

My Oceanography

MY
OCEAN-
OGRAPHY

HARRIET LEVIN

CavanKerry
PRESS

CavanKerry Press Ltd.
Fort Lee, New Jersey
www.cavankerrypress.org

Publisher's Cataloging-In-Publication Data
(Prepared by The Donohue Group, Inc.)
Names: Levin, Harriet.
Title: My oceanography / Harriet Levin.
Description: First edition. | Fort Lee, New Jersey : CavanKerry Press Ltd., 2018.
Identifiers: ISBN 9781933880679
Subjects: LCSH: Hesse, Eva, 1936-1970—Poetry. | Sculpture—Poetry. | Art—Poetry. | Ekphrasis—Poetry.
Classification: LCC PS3562.E88959 M96 2018 | DDC 811/.6—dc23

Cover artwork by Gray Jacobik
Book design and typesetting by Mayfly Design
First Edition 2018, Printed in the United States of America

CavanKerry Press is dedicated to springboarding the careers of previously unpublished, early, and mid-career poets by bringing to print two to three Emerging Voices annually. Manuscripts are selected from open submission; CavanKerry Press does not conduct competitions.

CavanKerry Press is grateful for the support it receives from the New Jersey State Council on the Arts.

Also by Harriet Levin

The Christmas Show (1997)

Girl in Cap and Gown (2010)

Creativity and Writing Pedagogy: Linking Creative Writers, Researchers and Teachers. (2014)

How Fast Can You Run, a Novel Based on the Life of Michael Majok Kuch (2016)

For Rick, Tedra, and Joshua

Endless repetition can be considered erotic.

EVA HESSE, *DIARIES*

I go down . . .
and there is no one
to tell me when the ocean
will begin.

ADRIENNE RICH, "DIVING INTO THE WRECK"

Contents

V. Deep Is Form

VI. Chain Polymers

VII. Axis Mundi

VIII. I Watch My Lover Pack

IX. Artifice

X. *The Road Between the Rims*

Note

These poems were triggered by the exhibition "Eva Hesse Sculpture," May 12–September 17, 2006, The Jewish Museum, New York. "Ringaround Arosie," "Ishtar," "Hang-Up," "Chain Polymers," "Ink Wash on Cardboard," "Just Before," "Contingent," "Laocoön," "Up the Down Road," "Eighter from Decatur," and "Oomamabooma" are titles of works by Eva Hesse. Some of the poems describe objects in Hesse's work and others imagine Hesse's life experiences—particularly her marriage at a young age to another artist and their early divorce. These poems are to quote Berryman, "essentially about an imaginary character (not the poet, not me) . . . who has suffered an irreversible loss and talks about (herself) in the first person, sometimes in the third, sometimes even in the second." Lucy Lippard's *Eva Hesse* (Da Capo Press, 1992) provided useful information along the way.

Lastly, this book is in memory of sculptor Brian Wagner who first introduced me to the work of Eva Hesse and lent me all his Eva books that I never had the chance to return.

I.

Hollow-Feeling, Covered in Spines

Ringaround Arosie

1965

You targeted me and forced my extinction,
drew circles around the parts of my body
where you dared to aim: my neck, my wrists,
my breasts. How could I escape your asteroid

come hurtling? Too much of my history
is etched in stone. Like lichen or mica,
you subsumed even my shadow
and sealed over the crevices

where I roamed. You drove long stretches of highway
and read my desires in strip-mining,
my sins exposed, determining
where to dig into the sediment's

repository of old arguments.
Jaw hardened, fist banging down,
you did not say *wait* or anything else
that broke into words of love,

because you wanted to render
a bee's hover and extract my DNA,
your artist's eye trained on the darkest nights
nothing but a chisel to pick away,

standing on top of that airless promontory,
bending over the rift to find a trace.
Measure my primitive atmosphere.
Preserve my dusky voice under glass.

Hollow-Feeling, Covered in Spines

On the cement steps
outside our apartment,
I found the black rail to grip.

Another time in the showroom
of a used car dealership.
American flags in plastic holders

waved from windows.
Under their banner
salesmen cleared the room,

brandishing cigarette lighters
from trouser pockets
with packets of menthols.

I did not slide
across buttery soft leather seats to feel
what the moment of travel

might offer,
or hug the wheel,
or vibe to music,

but under the spring glow bloom
of Acura's luminescence,
floor to ceiling glass walls,

blue sky roving through,
I practiced steeling myself,
longing for deliverance,

casting a metal mail coif
helm gorget, bevor, couter and gauntlet,
solid metal from my fingers to forearms

and toes to thighs,
as if bones no longer held
my body together,

but was mind-smithed,
constructed of metal.
Until that point,

the only armor I wore
was the gold ring
on the finger of my left hand,

so attached that I could not remove it
without soap and water,
twisting it over my knuckle,

careful to close the sink drain,
yet when it slipped off,
I chased it.

Humiliating me once more,
it rolled across the floor tile.
I crawled under my vanity

to retrieve it.
That was the night I could not bear
the stiffness on my finger,

could not bear to wash my hands
with my soap, handcrafted in Aspen
from tea tree and essential oils

to elevate my spirit. What dry earth,
what thunder might I summon
to rift it? What clouds to rise up,

to take me away
and begin again?
I growled, grew talons,

having grown so tired,
shrugging my shoulders
on a straight-backed chair.

Hang-Up

1966

A thin bent rod comes out of the frame.
There is no painting
in the frame,
just space penned in,
scarce and hardly there,
which is our awareness of it,
      white-knuckled, narrow, concealed. There must be something else there—
          some current visible in a more electric realm of filling
    lungs
with big gulps of air to withstand the rising shock.

An inside
out world of drenched skin
the full length of the whitewater,
the viewpoint both emptiness and *dependence upon the support.*
The crumbling schist at the confluence of rich salt springs,
where the artist
abandoned
knows deeply the demands of her work,
stretches her frames to over life-size,
        winds cloth over wood and steel
to wrap them
in the configurement
of mind
where the materials accrete.

Not a bench,
    just a couple
of slats of wood
nailed
    into a rusted girder.
Not a drawing, just lines
without shape

beribboning a page.
Not a self, just gradations of light
derived from the combinations.
The quiver in your voice
over the line

       as I lean in
hearing it, not hearing it
into my ear—beating of the drum,
oscillation of the hairs,
ridged from having held it.

Alarm

She dealt her pretty words like Blades

EMILY DICKINSON

I throw my miserable words
     like a pan hitting the linoleum.

Smoke stings my eyes. The chicken I cooked for him strewn across

the floor
         like a cloth fallen off someone's shoulder, the skin flayed,
     exposing blood and bone.

I am stripped, bare, felled, my body crashing like a tree,
struck by thunder,

rain falling in,
the window open
on this night. Rain wets the sill,
but nobody thinks to close it,
sweep up the chicken,
bend down with a moistened paper towel.
Rain falls through us,
splattering the floor,
like a body claiming its own,
the view clear to the pond
where the rain belongs,
if the rain were confined,
accumulating nutrients.
The refrigerator chirps
along with crickets
calling at dusk
from low in weeds,
a grating slow-pulsed song,
feeding our hunger—
ending too soon.

Ishtar

1965

You made me seek sleek alligator advances,
made me sleep, made me slough through
my own deep brown hair more machine than flesh,
the road washed out by rain all winter seeping.
Your hand on my knee set off alarms,
guards wielding pistols, dragging you to a dark
damp cell where you do not emerge walking
upright until after four million years to build
a dugout canoe and mudbrick, your ears
trembling with vibrations no one else can detect,
thinking you know all the meaning in the world
from featherweights in a ring, a camel's hump,
or bitumen leaking to the surface of a bubbling tar pit.
You took such big breaths when you climbed on top of me,
your lips demanding my commandeered head,
or you locked me in a soundproof prison,
no one hearing the noise I made to melt a glacier
and expose a sea shelf. You cannot imagine that rocky place.
It could have been different. You could have stopped
shocking me into life as you paced the carpet.
You barefoot and me forced to wear heels,
my legs chafed, my hamstrings torn.
I hated it when you called me Galatea,
hand-fed me candy corn left over from Halloween
shaped like a bullet grazing my head.
A night can be backfire's tambour or an argument
no one's willing to towel off. Times I walk the creek
and cup chameleons, proof of what defenses
nature gives lungs. Give me this: sea currents,
sea cliffs, a plunge so deep I reach the dead.
I know how you'd mourn for me.
Your sculptures bring in cash,

six or eight of them at a time, me stuck in your studio
with my breasts exposed, scavenging for food,
another invertebrate without a backbone,
my arms hollow-feeling, covered in spines.
If I didn't pose for you, you'd find someone else
with smoother skin to worship and become your lover,
while I stand at the seventh gate, denied my birth
in sea foam. You who have spilled crude,
I believed at first to be accidental, then lies,
absorbing infrared like those grotesque frogs
spawned in excess nitrogen no one will ever kiss.
I stand in your steamy breath's red tide.
Unlike those gaudy rubies you threw at me,
I cannot pawn its fumes rubbing the shore
to live. It destroys everything.
I wait for light cast in translucence,
a single stem in a glass bursting
until it flowers.

II.

Expanding the Picture Frame

Flesh

My husband's brushes, chisels, saws, bottles
of gesso and turpentine piled up in boxes.
The couch so worn out, its springs moan.

Cobwebs crumbled in the corners netting sound.
I pull my hair back into a ponytail
to gather each frayed wisp. I walk to the couch,

poke my elbows through the upholstery
and cup my chin in my hands.
The air smells so singed, I feel faulty,

about to slip and hit my chin on a corner
of his drafting table. From the other corner,
the face of another woman fills in for me.

The big clock on the wall syncs with her wristwatch,
cold and translucent, off by a few minutes,
as if entranced in her singular momentum.

He who motions for the two of us
to stand beside him to look at *Art Forum*
with the Lightning Field on the cover.

You've got to see this! he says—a four-page
color insert showing electrical currents emanating from rods,
one hundred and eighty during a storm,

the Sierra Madres engulfed in pink clouds.
The three of us stand there in a lull.
The sky gone white-silver. I read

meaningless sentences that stretch all the way
to the wall where he's bundled stacks of wood,
some of them gouged with wormholes

and scraps sawn off at odd angles,
raw material for his sculpture.
I touch the topmost board, draw tiny circles

as if it were flesh, bury my face
against my sleeve to breathe in the smell
of mineral spirits and gesso.

To be so permeated.
I'm addicted to that smell.
It's a smell I get when my work reaches magnitude.

But now it's ashes. It's toxic.
Now everyone I show my work
flicks dry grit off their fingertips.

Back in the light of day, in the room
where I paint with the windows over the river
and beneath, the sloping bank deep in mud,

they examine the page and question why I'm an artist,
as if such criteria exist—they can see it
roil and drift and urging me on.

Expanding the Picture Frame

Punching your fists in the air, you bleed under burnished light. I see the fight in you. I should have waited. Anyone else might have hid. I show you my paper on Carl Andre, his famous pronouncement that the view out a car window of the New Jersey meadowlands—floating miles of railroad yards, smokestacks, foxtail and goldenrod—depicts art. Both of us grew up one state over. Tons of ballast dumped in the marsh. Oil rainbows shimmering in streams. You tell me to return my books because I took them out with your card. You say they are overdue, denying me the courtesy of the grace period. You use your height and your weight to get me to work harder to inhale the thinner air. No gradual climb, just the unsupported stance that being with you demands. We sit on swivel stools side by side. To look at you eye-level means staring at your throat, my eyes treading the space where erupted our first spoken vows. Clear where the eyes might be. An opening for one of us to drag the other back to our shack, wake up with the sun and head out to sea in a dhow. You always say I'm not deep enough, that I'm, you know, shallow, caring about my hair, my animal body too much crescendo. I starfish flat and squeeze in.

Laocoön

1966

All touch,
that which springs

back, how grass was invented,
strands and strands

and wind,
so that things could start moving on their own

without being detected,
free even as a gaze.

Something shadowed,
like a caterpillar feasting on leaves.

I wanted to be a boy
who sat turned in the direction of his mother,

felt his way into sleep,
played with her hair.

I fidgeted, couldn't map
the noises that pulled me.

I twisted a strand, coiled it
around my finger, like rope tied

to mooring, and tugged on it,
forcing it to break.

Crush

Choose One –
Then – close the Valves . . .

    EMILY DICKINSON

He kept his eyes on me as if collapsing
the space between us, bringing the ceiling down
to its foundation, flattening the dimensions
of my thinking. The slow and deliberate way
he pulled back the plastic sheeting covering the marble
only an inch or two while he continued
holding my gaze, then abruptly turned his head
to stare at something else instead—some garbage cans
filled with refuse from his studio, curious
about the garbage and what it held.
He could turn it into art. It could become
part of his process, using it for his art.
Instead of working just one project,
he surrounded himself with another,
marble and refuse. The one still wrapped in plastic
ready to be moved and the one that's been
removed from floor, chair and bed—
my dusky voice, my half-smile—swept up, crushed.

Waterfall

Swirling round stones regardless the roaring,
edged sideways, your knees—can you bend them?

Can you hold the angle without becoming cramped?
Can you continually step down, fingers pushing back

hair in strands, a cascading, hurtling continuity
over basalt rock slopes? Imagine the fall, wheels in your heels,

birds, lilacs, laughter, your wings, your talons, your arms spread
to embrace the landscape's plowed fields,

cars swooshing past on the Interstate. Fall over stones
slip down to a trickle in a pool my body fills with

yours drop-by-drop icy cold at first then lukewarm
then aflame, ferns on the lower story, lilacs in the canopy

ringing rind and leaves. Such dampness seeps
from the edge of your boots, unless you remove them.

When I stand here I feel my limbs expand
like poses in yoga. The thunderous current

lifts my arms and knees.
I rise like a flock of starlings

scattering rhapsodies—the rigor, the truss,
the rib cage bursting through.

III.

Self-Study

Jacket

Shivering from the cold air
in the unheated studio,

I consider his mistress's denim jacket
slung across the arms

of his mechanical chair.
"Wear it," I permit myself,

commandeering air
like any tumultuous landing past excessive

temperatures of heat and ice.
Just as I am standing there, warming myself

in the jacket that my breasts and shoulders
barely fill, the material gaping cavelike

as if someone had suggested it
to clarify this contrast,

he bursts in, water running off his umbrella
and pouring down on the floor. He rushes over

to kiss me, opens his mouth and smiles up
at me and of course at the jacket

which covers me and my body,
metal snaps fastened shut.

Fine

Who weeps when mascara's fresh?
The tube I dig out from the pocket of my jeans,

the rearview mirror angled toward my face,
to lengthen my lashes, blacken them,

does not hide my terrible eyes.
The pile of books slides off my lap.

I scrunch down on the dirty floor
to retrieve them, rooting myself in darkness.

Books are overdue, bursting in their spines.
They extract a fine, the damp fibers ungluing.

Your Words

Parcel to this fall's assemblage,
  your words, bitter and cruel,
    dismiss bark and reject limbs.

Your words amass in slow release through my brain
  and I hear them
    crunching under heels cold and severed.

Savage words,
  no longer stone
    but rubble no longer wood but ash

no longer earth but sludge sheltering pane glass
  as rain rushes and rumbles.
    Your words and phrases pile up

on a bar deck during Oktoberfest,
  everyone having put down their drinks
    nighttime, the faraway moon,

while on the creek below,
  a kayaker dips his paddle
    in the water: your stirred-up words.

Your words are screeching, honking,
  rattling, flapping, whirling.
    I look up at the sky for ducks,

for iridescence baring itself,
  long necks twisting and craning.
    But the thing that's making this tremendous clamor,

this approaching onslaught so close
  that I get down on my knees
    and bow my head,

is only a landscaper's flatbed,
  two men in the cab poking their elbows
    out the windows, it's clattering engine,

shovels and shears that lurch forward
  then slide back to back.
    A migration this raucous

far off in the crystalline
  cloud-cover rife with cacophony.
    Words inscribed with these:

simple instruments,
  grass-stained, dull with use. A single cut
    releases the dying

limp and oozing,
  half buried and bruised as the truck,
    an old, rusted pickup veers

away, breaking down and emitting blame,
  leaking oil and black exhaust
    in feathery fumes.

Self-Study

Smudging the line where his lips lie, he kisses
and kisses me. I help him in his studio,
cook coconut chicken, wash his jeans,
but I resent every minute, like a rod
dipped in a brook, the fish squirming,
its jaws snapped shut. Or is it because
of what he made me feel with my hands,
the strength of the current—the rod and fish in my hands.
I lean over my tablet, its sizzling blankness,
for there is no space that does not rage:
snow in a bucket, canvas stretched over flatness.
I rip out the page in front of me, tear it
into pieces, leave nothing behind, not a single scrap.

Cold

The cold entered me, and I didn't want to go near him.
He opened my sketchbook.

I watched him flip through the pages,
squint, stare, smirk, his face a sky of phases,

not the full moon, not a parachute balloon,
because he bolted out the door.

I stood on the threshold struggling with the umbrella,
trying to open it without pinching the skin

on my thumb, while he was already outside
warming up the station wagon. The spring notch was stuck.

I couldn't do it. I opened it halfway,
like a gun on safety—a lack of courage—

and held it like that,
halfway open on top of my head.

IV.

Swimming in a Glass

Swimming in a Glass

Hardly anyone can stop looking through
the oversized martini glass made just for the disco.
It holds a girl in mermaid fins,
her breasts still sunlit and sparkling
with every eye riveted onto her, eels or hair
flickering in oscillation
under strobe and ultraviolet light,
black box and laser burst ball.
Her story will travel
from one country to the next.
An entire culture will spring up,
initiation rites constructed
around how long a girl can hold her breath,
lips puckered, that practice kiss, and heroically
reemerge, crook-necked against the glass toward a shore
of outstretched arms. It's easier to grow a culture

under glass. The most hermetic sound in techno
is percussion, not a hand drum made of skin,
but one that's forged with prerecorded sounds
like a fake ID, repeated on cue. Thank goodness
her story doesn't involve a raft,
machine guns, crossfire, a bloody massacre.
She can hedge death, flash like a gem
in glittering scales, the salt in the air, the spray
kicking back. She will always seek
as water seeks, a level, which, lacking confines
of a mortal life, ridiculously overflows,
a condition Hans Christian Andersen blamed on the mermaid's
attraction to drowning men,
their storms, endlessly battered loves.
Dancing with you, the hem of my jeans hits bottom.
Besides the threads of my clothing fraying,

my skin exposed, your fingers run a surge down my body,
so electric the current carries me.
I grow fins, numb and cold.
The low-pitched booms dolphins make
mouth to mouth fill up the universe.

Scylla and Charybdis

In my postcard from my vacation to the Caribbean, you point out the absence of corrugated metal roofs. Reed-thin dogs lick your wounds. Sink holes mean my liege, my pardon. Between us, the feud rages over the inhumanity of dairies. Days that are weaned cannot be repeated. I remember Dad's movies of tiny involuted limbs unfurled, afoot and amazed. Drunk milk makes me spill. I am beholden to the pail, the vessel, the container. All hemispheres of blessedness, which create an opening, fill with warmth. Instead, you use your bodies to hurl insults, bind yourselves to the fist, direct the tongues of their many-headed hydra, soggy, stained, spent. Yo, sisters, there was a time when tea brewed in our mother's kettle and each sip spoke honey, each hand sought the other to hold truth.

He Was Making a Mockery
of Our Relationship

Two shadows converge under a bridge
through clumps of bramble, high grass,
geese shit and reeds. The woman's shirt is off.
His head in her lap. She gropes around for her clothes.
Searching, she says to him that they should call it off,
but as I watch her snap her jeans,
squeeze her tits into her bra cups, hook and adjust the straps,
it seems like she wants to seduce both of us.

A tiny raindrop slips down from the sky,
more drops follow, a time of migration,
bird cries, their flapping wings.
His boots stomp down on earth as he runs after me
into the Art Workshop, steps in the geese shit.
The air inside vibrates with running saws—
another raw, migrating sound moving outward
and above us. The strong smell of arc welding
hammers at my head, narrows my senses.
Oxyacetylene releases its bitter burn.

He thinks he can get me to step
back toward him, unite under warm sheets.
He doesn't know that I learned
how to use perspective at a very young age.
Each piece of fruit
—the reddest apples from every view—
gathered in a clump on the coffee table,
the cuckoo clock chiming the hours,
taught me what to bring to life
and what to leave in the shadows.

Your Mind

I can read your mind, its static reaching me like downed cable wire hanging off
  a pole, sputtering in an upside-down caricature of compulsion.
I can read your mind, its loose-leaf binder rings holding a sheaf in its clasp,
  shackling words to the page, black ink expanding the margins.
I can read your mind, its deteriorating tree looming within the circumference
  of its range, toppling onto the roof of a house, crashing through its walls.
I can read your mind cordoning off the water behind its towrope, the taut strands
  speciously separating the shallow end of the ocean from its enormity.
I can read your mind, its Morano glass bubbling over a flame, blown into a
  preconceived shape, unwilling to risk amorphousness.
I can read your mind, its black brushstrokes winding down from the top, its
  craggy hills and figments of streams foregrounded in a Chinese painting.
I can read your mind, its signature confined to a corner, a jagged scrawl
  authenticating the macabre shape of your aura.
I can read your mind, its sullen alphabet, like the incomplete circle of the letter
  C, about to, poised, nearness exaggerated.
I can read your mind, its swimmer bowing its head then lifting it as its
  breaststrokes sling it from wall to wall.
I can read your mind, its whelk inside a shell, its shoulders stuck in the process
  of twisting, like an ammonite fossil 70 million years old reconstructed to
  show the comparison between the living and the extinct.
I can read your mind, its hand carrying a duffel bag filled with rifles to be fired
  in exchange for separatism, its beard unshaven, its beret askew.
I can read your mind, a disturbed hornet's nest releasing its swarm in
  cartoonlike revenge, darting out of a hollow—needling through my core.

Heat Field

I jab the sharp point beneath my thumbnail,
then snap the pencil in half, like the cigarette
you refused to light for me. You lit one for someone else,
inserted it in the crook of her fingers.
It gave off little sparks, swift, sharp,
aligning the two of you.
I stood apart, apart from your heat field,
unladen, before the first snow, like driving in
from the outskirts and seeing the city's skyline
shimmering through treetops, leafless, bare-limbed.

V.

Deep Is Form

Statuesque

A crane and a wrecking ball out
in the open. No other way
to take him down. I've tried to correct him,
dismantle him, reconstruct him

in a dream of slipping into
the graveyard at night and assembling
body parts, electricity
firing up synapses, mechanical limbs

clanking, just one more monster
in the architecture of mind.
He's so tall, his belly is obstructed
by skyscrapers. The dew gathering

on his neck hovers over the city
like a cloud. Birds hunch on his shoulders—
crows, ravens and vultures—grim like gargoyles.
Before there was sky, nothing towered.

Earth stood at bedrock infused
with the mineral sense of fire
and strata rifting and crumbling.
I cannot restore him to life.

Cold is the shadow that drapes his
spine. Somewhere beneath lies flesh,
rippling rapid. Crushing twigs and petals,
all edifice collapses.

Urban Myth

A projection straight from my roiling mind's swamp:
at an intersection in Palm Beach Gardens, a fourteen-foot long alligator
stops traffic, its tail swinging out from behind its body
not thrashing so much as flat-bottomed squiggling,

viewed through windshields—accelerated, mechanized.
I cannot deny it. No longer paranoia but a real
reeling monster equipped with a toothy smile
and tender oscillating eyes.

Before my encounter, I was flipping through pages,
seeing whose address I'd come to by chance.
A gentle wisp could proffer a shortcut
to sainthood, build a nest of a name pinpricked with light.

You said we should talk. A lot of things get said over the phone,
but never in person, the cord buckling.
Is *hi, how are you?* truly preferable to that surge
of sweet dark Ghirardelli cut into squares,

confection infiltrating defenses?
Garish, cartoonish, festooned in scales, claws, and teeth—
ours, salient. This is what saturates the sky at sunset,
a twinge's blood-red hue. Prowess merges

with the throttle of diesels, my stop-and-go attempt
at wrestling an instinct only to tie rope around its jaw
and trap it back into its cage—still reeling from the impact,
it brought me to my knees.

Bumming a Cigarette

I pretend to read as if the words on the page (Carl Andre's *Cuts)* are more important than the voices in my husband's studio. I hear one of his fellow students—a girl with shiny otter hair all spun around—ask him for a cigarette, when the girl could have asked others, those sitting beside me, making letters out of smoke. Not a smoker myself, I can't read the curlicues before they dissolve, don't know their language, their languid gauge. *A girl reached him, her hipbones were sharp* . . . that is how their story is going to begin. He rips open the cellophane on a new pack, peels it off like the shirt over his head, the jeans on his legs and inserts a cigarette in the crook of the girl's fingers. They align and produce a current. They're glowing, the two of them, they're so attracted. I'm standing on their periphery. They feel me opposing them, trying to poke through. The silver face of a dime sparkles on the floor. High cheekbones and upturned nose look too valuable to leave behind. I think about picking it up before anyone else grabs it. Should spend it, mark the outline on a patch of prairie, set fire to it. Resting my hand on one of the power saws until I see how close to the blade I've placed it, I sashay toward him, pull a cigarette from his pack and snap it in half.

My Oceanography

A strand of algae leaves its rubbery
translucent swatch on my skin. My first impulse
is to peel it off lest a horror
movie version of contagion unfold
and my skin turn zombie green—telltale alien,
more slime than flesh, attracting gnats, pinhead skitters
moving so rapidly all is flux.

My second impulse is to keep it as a totem
of subterranean life, a scrap chiseled
from things that are meant to sink. Deep is form,
like a snail that burrows into silt, shell
growing out of sludgy cravings.
A life-in-death feel. The croaks frogs make
drowning in natural desire. Believe me,
diving into this mosh pit, I do not
float softly through water.

Pond life is too shallow. No flotsam or jetsam,
sneakers, ice-hockey gloves, Chinese message
in a bottle. Even the dam's stopped up,
no bigger than an oversized sink filled
nightly with dishes. No reputable
oceanographer will chart its depth—
another thing I'll never know
about myself. Territorial and fiercely defensive,
rock bottom will not be reached.

To be essential something must be both deep
and wide. Eyes with skies in them. Upswept
lashes and brows. A western monsoon.
Dreams that stretch over many nights to mimic
the feel of sea-foam on ankles,
down to the cellular properties of summer.

Current

He twirls a bicycle tire between his hands,
slows it down with practiced control

and whirls his index finger along the rubber edge.
Sunlight strikes the metal rim, heats it up

with foundry heat to the point of melting.
He leans back and presses his hips against me.

His hands cup both my breasts.
The surge runs off his fingers—

flickers crashing slow,
another kind of flow.

A helicopter's exhausted whirl.
Purple lupine covering fields

stretched out into a human shape,
a body with bumps and declivities—

an aluminum "No Trespassing" sign hammered to a tree.
Just the tips of our boots getting wet.

VI.

Chain Polymers

Chain Polymers

The days we spent in Northern Arizona opened me up to my worst and least fears. If someone asked me how to slur, how to be drunk, before that trip, I'd have told them to snake around people and flail on the floor. That's how people I knew acted. But after that trip, I'd have said something totally different. People drink to forget. I held that trip sacred. The places we went to were sacred. The Petrified Forest. Canyon de Chelly. Walnut Canyon, The Acoma-Zuni Trail. Even if I was piss drunk, I'd still remember them, the Fiat's tires permanently stained with the red dust from the road.

Once we found the highway, a barren route bristling with sagebrush, my husband drove in the left lane, accelerating to pass construction trucks and oil tankers. The vista enormous, flat land stretched hundreds of miles in each direction. Back East, trucks are sequestered to the slow lanes, but here they amble along at over eighty miles an hour, jostling and churning, half mechanized, half live animal.

We drove in silence for a long couple of minutes listening to a commercial for a restaurant in Gallup called Taco Casito. He bent the fingers of one hand against the steering wheel and cracked his knuckles. Something about that motion called attention to itself. It had to do with the way he held his cigarette in the crook of his fingers.

At first, I sensed a single flame. Then I took in the whole spectrum. All I could think about was my husband cheating on me and why was he with me in the first place, when I had no standing in the department, not even a fellowship? Or was I some kind of man trap? I was a vagina with teeth, an evening person. I lolled around in bed with my T-shirt hiked up and my breasts exposed, last night's dinner dishes piled up on a nest of vegetable peels heaped in the sink. And those times when I'd get so anxious, and couldn't paint and needed to talk, I'd force him to sit beside me on the couch in his studio and spend the whole evening with him listening to me rant on and on, as if depriving him of studio time was my plan for wrecking his career.

I felt wretched and terrified. I saw a sign for the old Highway 66 and told him to take it on a hunch. My father and stepmother traveled on Highway 66 in 1960 on their honeymoon. They slept in a motel called The Wigwam. There's a picture of it in their scrapbook. It shows a circle of fiberglass structures large enough for a person to walk inside. Under the picture, they pasted a caption that read, "Have you Slept in a Wigwam Lately?"

We were stopped on the roadside when a dark blue Jeep Cherokee slid over the gravel. A guy in his early thirties, he was dressed in garb, a fringed buckskin shirt and moccasins with rawhide laces. He looked like he was en route to a ceremony. Most of the people we had seen outside the pueblos wore faded jeans and T-shirts. He slowly walked over. "Ho," he called from several feet away.

Up close, I could see his face more clearly, his forehead lined. It was like seeing something come into focus only to make you less certain you know what it is, the way after working hours on a drawing, you're not any more certain of where it's taken you.

"You're on Indian lands here," he said. He told us that if we didn't get off we'd be incarcerated. "The Tribal Council will impound your car. You don't want that to happen. You'll never get it back. They'll take it for a joyride over the canyon." He pointed across the hills. "It's a junkyard down there. Mostly auto parts."

My husband and I told him we hadn't known and that there weren't any signs, and he said that everyone knows where the lands begin and end and what's Indian and what's white and that if we had a map of the territory, he'd show us. I thought of our map wedged into the crack between the driver's seat and the console, still wrapped in cellophane, lined with thick folds, and of our guide books with the pages folded in to mark the chapter called "Driving Notes" and "People of the Southwest" under our gear in the trunk.

"You can visit these lands, but not without a guide. I can take you through in the morning. Ever see the movie *Billy Jack*?" he asked.

We had.

He told us that these were the lands where they shot the movie. We looked around in amazement. "We got a couple of good things out of it," he said. "A library. A museum. I got to be an extra."

"What do you like to do?" he asked and extended his hand and introduced himself. "Edwin Torres, registered Navajo guide. I could take you through Acoma

Pueblo if you'd like, but you seem like people looking for something different, a different kind of encounter." He shot my husband a look.

We told him we were trying to find land art and asked him if he could take us to see *The Lightning Field*.

"*Lightning Field*?" he said, crossing his arms over his chest and shaking his head. "That's not on Indian land. But okay." He stepped across the loosely packed earth to the passenger side of the car, where tiny pinpricks of light shone through the dust coating the windshield, all soot covered now. He kicked the tire with his foot. "You should be driving four-wheel," he said. "Your car is worthless here."

I looked at my husband. Dusk was closing in. "The lodge is down a little ways," Edwin said. "Right on the Acoma-Zuni Trail. You can stay there for the night and I can take you on the trail in the morning in my Jeep, that is if you're up for the experience." The way he emphasized the word experience reminded me of boys in high school who dealt drugs. There was always someone in our crowd you could go to and get some speed or a Quaalude even if you didn't have any money. I hoped he wasn't a diversion sent this way by the woman my husband had been cheating with.

"An experience?" my husband asked. "We'd be very interested in an experience," he said. Clearly, my husband didn't have second thoughts. If I'd objected, I'd have ruined it for him.

The next morning, before dawn, Edwin rapped on our door. "I'm here," he shouted.

We piled into his Jeep and he took us to a creek at the bottom of a mountain where psilocybin grew. A crowd of mushroom gatherers dipped their hands in the creek water to rinse off the dung from the mushrooms they'd collected. Smoky clouds of fecal matter floated on the surface.

Edwin squatted and shined his flashlight over the grass. Up close the stench was more putrid, more sour. He poked his index finger into heaps of cow manure. He shined his flashlight on reddish mushrooms with white specks. "*Amanita muscaria*," he said, "they're fatal. Don't worry, I've studied *muscaria*. I took an herbology class in college." He stopped and fixed his eyes on me, savoring my reaction. "Just joking. I took several courses."

His words froze in my brain. Except for his clothes—a buckskin jacket and moccasins—he didn't look Navajo. My husband sat cross-legged, completely relaxed, grinning from ear to ear. "Aren't you worried?" I asked him.

"Relax," he said. "Look around. Look, where you are."

The sun had come up. I could see the cows on the next plateau, their spotted flanks. The red earth. "Does he know what he's doing? Is he really Navajo? We could die from this," I said.

He put his finger to my lips. "Shhhhh. Don't let him hear you." He sprawled out on the grass. "Just go with it. Float on the flow."

Relatives I'd never met, survived on mushrooms when they hid in the forest during the War. One survived three winters, crediting the boots she grabbed last minute, the toes peeping out through the open closet door in the hallway of her house in Borszczów, with saving her life. How did she learn to discriminate the poisonous mushrooms from the safe ones, or was she willing to take the risk for the lure of tasting something moist in her mouth? I got freaked out whenever I found myself in situations that resembled theirs. I couldn't avoid it. I kept falling into them. It was too late to get out of there.

Edwin climbed up the bank and laughed. He swiveled his hips around as if he was a woman and sung the first few bars of "Stand by Your Man." After he sorted through the mushrooms, Edwin asked what we wanted to accomplish on our trip. Edwin said it was important to set the agenda before we got started and asked us to meditate on it for a couple of minutes. My husband told Edwin that he'll use this trip to feed his art.

"Now that's what I call an enlightened agenda," Edwin said. "It's not money or success you're worried about, it's creating the art."

"It's not fair. It's not fair," I repeated to myself. My husband's work always came before mine. I wasn't about to let that happen again. I told Edwin that I was dissatisfied with my work and that I wanted to use the trip as a focal point for breaking through. I told him that I needed to be more flexible and that the trip would help me loosen up more. Edwin said that a lot of artists got closer to their individual styles from doing hallucinogenics and that my quest was a good one. He said that he believed that making art was contingent upon a liberated mind.

My husband said, "Look, both of us need to be free. Look what that fellowship contest did to you. Made you cut your hair short."

I ran my hand through it. My head sweated at the scalp line. "That's not the reason why I cut it."

"Yes, it is," he said. "All that thick black curly hair."

"No, I was angry."

"I know why you cut it."

I stepped away. "You don't know a thing about it."

"Whoa, okay," Edwin said, "It's beautiful hair. It's an honor to stand here and look at it." Edwin took off his hat. He bent over. He didn't have any hair. "An honor," he repeated.

"That's because you're bald," I said. He winked his eye at me.

"It's beautiful, man," my husband said.

"You're an artist, you ought to know," Edwin said.

What business was it of Edwin's? I wished he hadn't mentioned anything about my hair. He pulled a jar of honey out from his satchel and poured it into a flask without spilling a single drop down the sides. He tossed in a handful of the chopped-up mushrooms. Shaking the flask and pouring some of the amber-colored concoction into a tumbler, he told us to drink it.

Edwin smiled and said, "If we were back at my house, I'd mix this with a blender." He held the tumbler while we sipped at it. I wondered if I should drink less because I'm only five foot three and they're over six feet, but no one pointed that out. Edwin waved his hand in the air. Filled with ragged sagebrush and rock, the air felt prehistoric, the canyon bathed in silence.

Edwin squatted down on the ground with us. This other guy, a white person in his early twenties, an artist maybe or someone who just graduated from college without a job and nowhere to go, came over and asked if he could join in. He wrapped us in a bear hug as if he'd known us for years.

Edwin mumbled something under his breath. His face got so red the veins stuck out on his neck. He poured another tumbler but drank it all himself, without offering any to the guy. After he finished drinking it, he held the tumbler upside down over the grass for the last dregs to drip out.

The guy's shirt was belled at the sleeves like a suitcase with expandable flaps. Edwin flashed him a frozen smile. The guy sprung forward from his knees toward Edwin, but Edwin pushed his legs out and the guy tripped over them and plunged into the creek. The water level was deeper than I had supposed. I could see the guy's head, chest and shoulders stick up like an animal mired in a trough. The noise that came from him sounded like a squeal, changing the resonance in his throat to a higher pitch. The sound became so high that after it was over, I thought that there were dogs somewhere that could still hear it.

Edwin glared at me as if I were the cause.

"Who is he?" I said.

"Forget him," Edwin said.

"What do you have against him? Who is he?"

Edwin didn't answer. He squinted his eyes to look me up and down, convinced I had something to do with it, something about my clothes or my body. He was a master at manipulating people to accomplish his goals, adopting that lustful male predator's gaze that reduced me to a fuck object.

I hid my hands behind my back, afraid of what I might do with them and why was I the only one who heard her father say from his seat in front of the TV, *Can't you walk like a lady?* I was going to clamor out of there, make as much noise as Devonian fish growing new fingers and hands from their fins to breathe in air.

VII.

Axis Mundi

Whir

Summer, the dominion
of crickets, music that can never be seen,

never be reached. Inside the workshop,
I'm running the miter saw,

cutting 1x2s to make frames,
the blade whirring steadily.

The jagged music of the blade
up on its knees, spinning all the way around

and back again,
like water carrying its depth.

Shoeless and shirtless, sunlight beats down,
making me squint, groggily.

Up the Down Road

1965

I know that you know that I'm the better artist
but you had me convinced
that you were better. You had the bigger studio,
the fellowship, the windows facing the rainbow,
the sky turned ultraviolet, after the tornado.
Weather, too, bestowed upon you prizes,
gave you the retina of an oriole while I got shook.
Fish nibbled at my feet—big pucker fish
in water too murky to see their stripes—and it rained.
I remembered to grab a tree trunk and hug it,
get down on the deck with bits of leaves peppered flat to it,
the wind dancing itself into a frenzy, tapping me
like the drunk at a party, his mismatched socks showing.
Yet, holding a fellowship marked you
as someone to watch. In that way, we were the same,
only I was the one shoplifting sable hairbrushes
at Utrecht because they were too expensive,
even with my in-state tuition reduction.
You were on a stipend, you said,
that could afford you luxuries: hand mannequins,
oil primed linen, sea salt infused chocolates,
exotic fruit plates heaped with mangoes.
At Open Studios, Dominque and Levy
(friends of the department head) walked in
and bid for your paintings, whispered at their altar,
while I scrambled eggs with piri-piri powder,
scattered shells in our compost, preparing you a welcome
like the first meal the pilgrims ate at Plymouth,
after disembarking and setting their feet down
on land. I still love to cook, you could not sour
my tongue, my meat or my bones, despite my hand racing

to record all the phases of our breakup in charcoal,
this cold spring among willows, before stuffing my clothes inside a suitcase,
snapping its jaws shut and wheeling it into the night.

Axis Mundi

Where in the church of the mind,
the mind's sawn down trees,

where hardwood's stacked up,
quartered and milled, where under the nave

the painting is placed,
in the left-hand side aisle,

the viewpoint from which one approaches the altar
do the putti recover us and give us wings?

The figures are over life-size,
their heartbeats thump through the church

in the direction of the brushstroke,
drift at the edge of fields left to the shape it takes.

Sometimes it's rain the reach of rain.
Sometimes it's purer, less mixed. Jubilance.

I felt it running down the hill in the rain
running so as not to get wet but getting wet.

Pause to tie my shoelace,
as if, tying it, I might actually pull together—finding it undone.

Contingent

1968

Wrapped   concealed   hinged   railroad tracks

muddy   red-tinged   sidling up to the rim

an unfinished world of gallops   across sagebrush

something absurd   exaggerated   repeated   a herd

scaled down within a boundary   malleable

each nerve's jangled core   will I muster

the confidence to roam   to expand in terraces

far beyond the goosebumps on my skin?

there is this chill in the room   this clammy feeling

the humidity curls my hair   flings salt in my face

dissolves in my lungs   to keep me adrift on

these waves flecked with sun   some forces bear down

throttle the breath   the *th* activated   as in the drug

no place to go other than this   steep-sided   foaming white rapids

Appetite

No longer a marshmallow poked through a stick.
Too short to hang onto.
Once, gooey was honeyed.
This is before reality melts under
my face and hands.
The man who becomes my lover gives me the stick,
making his way straight to me.
I take the stick from him and blow on the flames
and wave the marshmallow in the air
until, cool to touch, I slide it off.
The soft, sweet warm taste of the marshmallow,
tinged with the taste of fire
clings to me, his ghost-glue on my lips.
So this is how a presence becomes material,
strikes sparks, some twisting together,
(his jacket lying crumpled up on a milk crate.)
"Put it on," he says, waving entry. "You're cold."

VIII.

I Watch My Lover Pack

Bloodthirsty

My husband looks at his mistress's naked body.
Noxious nail polish fumes leap
around the room. She closes her arms around him,
misplacing the lid, but with the bottle
in her hands, it spills down onto her breasts

and down her crotch and legs to
the secondhand Tibetan carpet where it spills
over the borders and across rare hand-spun lilies
turning her into the bloodthirsty monster
she had teased him about, as if she'd taken a bite
out of his neck and blood dripped out her mouth
onto the threadbare carpet, beneath to the floor,

pooling on the ceiling of the apartment below,
the way a bathtub faucet drips
and depletion rusts the rim.
She leans back, the polish in blotches
on her skin. In view of her hunger,
he hears her say "bloodthirsty" and snort through the scent,
and he sees the viscous in her eyes
each time he rubs the towel across her breasts,
down to her thighs, her eyes glazed over watching him intently,
the bottle empty, its brush spread wide enough.

Deity Fossil

I watch my lover pack, feel my breath
become used up. I help him leave, tell him
to go, ingrained in that gesture—
survival in the strictest sense. I who
finish off the bottle of whiskey
he leaves behind, I who in raising
the bottle hold to my lips day spilling
into night, the end of the Mesozoic,
the exhuming of bones, the turning
of leaves, wind churning,
beginning in the creases of a sheet.

Ink Wash on Cardboard

What wholeness can I
hold in my hands?
Ice and a glass?
A glass and its transparency?

Gallant, a pack animal
might unload me
far from city lights.
Unless I can carry herself
over to the next yard, over the tops

of mansard roofs
and stop focusing on my
own house and my own roof,
I will never create
an unobstructed view.

The backyard overgrown
with everything that is brought to it,
mostly mind. I am no longer
in the mind of love.
There is no opening unobstructed

to see beyond. So maligned
so suddenly does it depart,
rises and leaves, a rustle, a flutter.
The darkness asserts its lack of clarity,
unmeasured, disordered, veiled,

keeping out morning.
The missing morning has been severed
from the outside world,
penned up in stone.
Such obsessive thoughts bore down,

stay in the forecast.
Storms stay in the air.
Things get flung, get broken, shatter.
No eye in the storm gets shut.
Holes get carved into rock outcropping.

Goth Girl Fallen on the Floor

Once she licks salt
off the rim,
her thirst grows
for monkey's
business—peanuts, sawdust, and demure
poses mimicking the barstool's red swivel,
ardor so intense
it must constantly spin.
Expand   expand   she wills herself.
She leans off-balance
to recenter herself
toward the outermost
edge, the studded spiral of what stirs, shakes and dislodges.
That she is dressed in spandex
keeps her muscles looking rippled.
Her stiletto
spikes the floor, pins down her sidestep,
her sideslip—the spilled drink, the bumped chin, the bit lip.
Now she admonishes herself
over her chipped
tooth and glass.
Her clenched face
needs the breath
of a blower to shape
rim to rim.
Tables are set or taken away.
These things appear in rotation.
Earth itself
gauges an overflow
There are tears.
She is almost halfway out the door,
then turns to face the mirror
knowing what is shown there

is in reverse
and opposite.
Turned backs
point their barbs
from the absurd
distances of stars.

Just Before

This was before the cockle head's shadow
crept across my shelf. Soft, the sheets I lay on.
Naked I lay amid a mecca of bird choirs,
chway clee-ip cleeer,
before X-ACTO knife cuts dragged
across canvases and stinging hot liquid
spilled onto my thighs, chiggers bore into my skin,
the eggs they deposited, the larvae.
And if life seeps through like dirt under a fingernail,
hammers me back into place—
telltale the nails—and succeeds in retrieving me,
every morning I brew coffee, the sound
of the pot percolating will roar like thunder
and the house shake to its foundation
while the coffee drips into the pot.
Every morning the same teaspoons spread out
on linen like a faceless corpse.
All that Spanish moss clinging to the living
vine—shoeless and naked from the waist down.

Oomamaboomba

1965

I've had to stop saying that boy's name.
It lay between *sparrow* and *sorrow*,

tipping its weight, shadowing water,
deviating from true north to project

in undulating lines at the base
of my throat—exhausted, peeled, stretched

like tea leaves stuck in the weave
of a paper towel. And if I haven't

said it well or loudly
enough, then I don't want

that kind of love.
So spare me no mercy.

IX.

Artifice

Rebuke

Somehow depleted with her breath, the failing light of the park lies silted at
the bottom.
Besides the pain that inundated her body, dove in its spike, she felt an
elemental fear,

spitting fire, roots singed through deep layers of sediment. Nothing pushes off,
is dipped deeply without drowning, face down, barely breathing,

inundated in water, no murkier element to slip into. The force, the displaced air,
delivers the park, that panic preserved, unyielding, diving headlong, frenzied,
bruised,

desiring bottomless motion, like being handcuffed to the bottom of a table,
hot metal
burning deep wounds into her flesh. My dive, in the millisecond between breaths,

somehow shifts my body into park, whirls me into a sixth dimension, the element
of imagination made fluid. Naked, unclothed, immersed, rebirthed to the
elemental,

blameless, guiltless, bottom-to-top, inlaid like a parquetry where both the
living and
dead lie entwined, depth perception granted, my breath stopped in her lungs, my

nakedness her divestiture. Disease dive-bombed her cells. Less the elements
that have always lain dormant than the pain of breathing. As I slide to the bottom,

a kind of domino reaction, an avalanche of depth, the unendurable blossoming,
I feel this day at the park. I don't stay with the others on the plateau. Breathless,
I rush

from the bottom to throw rocks against the sign that reads Belmont Park.
The diagonal of my dive cuts deep arcs, intersecting with a hidden element.

In Service to a Bird

My bicycle chain hangs off its gear wheel.
I bend down to fix it,
my hands smudged with black grease,
my bicycle repaired and ready to ride,
matching the sun's rays stride for stride—my deus ex machina
conjured up from revolving mind chambers
through the narrow slit
of a door, speaking body language,
seeing the jeweled facets on the stone,
the broken-down state
that often looks beautiful—half repaired, half slipshod.

Judgment

Everybody could see it—
but it was you

who dropped your eyes over the page
to roam around the drawing.

You grinned and cocked your head, "Nothing.
I don't see anything."

You turned the page sideways
as if to correct it. "Nothing," you repeated.

A dime sparkled on the floor.
I picked it up before you did

and hurled the money, insignificant
as it appeared.

Thrown, or simply underfoot,
no more value given to the things I make.

I pulled the sketchbook out of your hands
and carried it across the room,

turning the page clockwise and close up
for a different time zone and sunlit sky,

mumbling loud enough for you to hear,
"How dare you? How dare you?"

Stone

As his furious words cannot be taken back,
my gorgon lids grow heavy.

My hair of living snakes sheds beneath his bed,
feeds larvae on his sheets.

Hateful to be tracked to the smell
of ginkgo cell by cell.

Hateful to envy the cupped blossoms of tulips,
deeper and redder sunsets,

the release lever on pinball. *O the cry*
did knock against my very heart!

Indignant as snow, a towel for a lampshade,
candles for wickedness.

With the grind of each flung
shoe against the wall my fangs sharpen.

All my precious slingbacks and chunkies
cease not to make him cower,

the cloven toes, heels and sole he once carried
across the threshold like a bride.

Artifice

He tucks a strand of hair behind his mistress's ear,
"Hold it! Stop right there,"
I yell. "Keep your hand where it is, don't move."
Then I zip open my backpack
and take out my sketchpad filled with nameless
people drifting in and out, forms drawn
in big, quick strokes collapsing into shadow.

Hunger

Before he walked into the middle
of the room and spoiled everything,
she found in it
a pasture for horses.
Smell of uncut grass,
dirt tamped down.
She wanted to lie in it forever,
lie down and sleep,
but he entered, clapping his hands
and she was struck by the power
of his infatuation,
the hunger. He reached
for the *Art Forum*
and turned to the centerfold.

"The invisible is real," he said, quoting from the text.

He kept his eyes on the page.
He studied her for a moment, then said,
"You need to get used to people criticizing your work."

"That's the problem, I am used to it."

"Then you need to grow thicker skin."

O she should have been stark and obdurate
among spewed chunks of stone,
structures fallen on their sides,
absorbing rain and heat, not a pasture at all
but a field split like a hoof,
torn down the middle,

the way her ribs bunch up into buttresses
around her chest,
this place she's come to
now marked on her body—
hunger keeping its teeth strong, its ribs lean.

X.

The Road
Between the Rims

Daylight Savings

The hours swim across the Pacific
and land at the International Date Line

to free all the lost hours of travelers
shadowing the ocean.

The hours feel their hearts ache
because they cannot fly

with the precision of jets arriving
on an imaginary landing strip with open doors.

Their words cannot reverberate with the sonic
boom of dolphins, even in the chambers

of the most hallowed judges.
They mostly tick and chime

and trumpet baroquely immune
to gunfire, cuckooing

not with the whistle of a real bird,
just a carving opening its wings and beak.

The hours witness fear
like pumpkins and scarecrows.

For a while, the hours stop her face from wrinkling
and restore her to beauty, but they tire

of her narcissism and refuse to continue standing still.
They channel their voices and squawk at her,

tempting her dog to chase them. Wrapping his leash
around her wrist, she maneuvers her legs to hold him

back while he tugs and pulls,
until just as he is breaking away, they grant her

one more hour. She wakes early to sunlight
and kicks off her quilt. Shivering,

she wanders downstairs to the door.
It's like the time a lover

gave her one hour at Filene's Basement
to fill her arms. Only now, the knob gives off sparks.

Rebellious, it threatens her to touch it.
How can she build a nest in leaves

and give gratitude for the hour
if she is greeted by nothing but metal? It will be hard.

Smoke

If I could use smoke as a medium,
I'd have no trouble creating great art.

Strands of clove-scented smoke pull me in layer
by layer amid the mesmerizing sound

of rain hitting the roof,
sidling across the windshield and draining off the hood.

I tilt my head back and imagine
a cigarette pressed against my lover's lips.

Three more left in the pack.
This is the last of him.

Smoke fills my mouth,
passes down my throat and into

my lungs where it infiltrates
every cell in my bloodstream.

I smoke past the red line on the tip,
his body's imprint—

jawline, nape, neck—
tuck the stub into my jean's pocket

for his scent to seep through,
linger, live in my pocket as a remnant,

as I throw open the car door,
step forward and out of him.

Eighter from Decatur

1965

To squeeze your body
into the struts of a train's underside

all through Brenner Pass,
is to hear wolves keen,

feel wind thrum along your spine,
and witness log pines descend into the valley,

the ones still standing, their long, sleek trunks,
and the ones that have been felled,

grass poking through their ribs,
because you are still a child

and will not remember
anything except the frontiers

of twisting vines and leaves,
cold, dark, hunched into yourself

believing goodbye is the name of a place
where you will one day return,

your body shocked into rails, wheels
and the piston pumping inside your chest.

The Road Between the Rims

The badminton racket is a manifestation of myself, lying deep
down in the bottom of a creek. The kind that snaps back, taut.
Resilient, strong enough to strike and smash a birdie.

I walk around to the back of the building and peer in through the windows.
Wood floors, metal desks, a chair on metal coasters, an orange extension
cord bundled into the corner. There I am again, wound up, back in the moment,

shock and aftershock. The wind bores through me.
Swaying branches make a cleft in the road, forge a route.
I used to want a souvenir—maple syrup, maple candy,

maple sugar, everything's maple in Vermont, or one last cappuccino
in the café, but I don't now. Now I defer to the weather, to blankness
spuming and the gas station attendant's oily hands when I ask for change.

When I was keeping myself away from poetry, getting manicures and haircuts,
I'd open up bottles of nail polish in different shades and brush them on,
then remove them, until I couldn't decide which color I wanted.

After the manicurist massaged my skin with oil,
she fitted me with gloves—the final sword thrust in the bull's hide.
Money cusped the conversation, a clavicle supporting its neck and head.

A pickup parked in the driveway. The house facing me with all its blinds.
I hope the driver won't haul away the junk that's been accumulating in the yard.
Wood scraps, blackened garden gloves, cracked terra cotta, ice skates, wagons.

That's the stuff I like to think about. Whose gloves were they
and do they still mold to skin? Someone's essence arrived at by focusing on the gloves,
earth ground in. The things someone might throw into a fire

to listen to the sizzle and restore oneself to reason. So the
gloves, pelted with flames, turn out to be inflammable.
Reason is not restored—there I am again.

The Weight of His Body Rested Mainly on One Leg

for R.P. (1960–2012)

The place I find to work in is cold,
the thermostat turned down.
Filled with disarming judgments,
the blank canvases face me.

I turn away from them
the way I once turned from my brother
when he ripped clusters of Queen Anne's
lace from the forest floor

to plant them on our lawn.
"Weeds," my father said. Next summer
they multiplied across the grass
and grew reflected in my brother's face in the storm door

and he could not rip them out
without taking his own life.
I pick up a sardine can
and tear off its label, wanting

no identifier, no name
to name it, stop it from becoming.
I fill the inside with spring coils
and solder them, a tangle

of nerves, a jangle of
tentacles, a constant reaching
from underneath, up to a
surface, without knowing for what—

that the state of matter is whirling,
a momentum, encrusted with salt.
I'm reaching for a joyful way to be in it,
slipped through fluttering to life,

repeating the process again and again,
its rough sketch, contour and color, shadow
and sprinkling light—O my brother!
I soldered some spring coils to a can.

Just soldered them.
How they work together,
mollusklike, spinning pearls,
drifting in and out of the liquid epoxy—

My Water Bottle

Croix-de-Bouquet, Haiti

The real thing he pulled was greater than the water bottle
turned toy—bottle cap wheels attached to a string—
as it followed behind him across the cracked cement.

In it had been rivers and rain. The strong force of a waterfall.
A stream winding through certain bodies. Another child came running out
the door asking to play with it. I watched the string exchange hands,

loop a finger as the children outran it and their creation rolled,
wobbled, tipped forward on its neck.
The speckled wings fluttered and rose, even as I hid somewhere

in my childhood basement, my mother shouting from the kitchen
to pick up all my toys scattered from their boxes,
toys I held in the darkness of night, clutched close in whispers.

The child without any stood beside me, followed me around,
stayed near, waited until my last sip and my bottle was empty.
He tapped it lightly and my heart burst. It took time

for me to understand. What did I not offer?
The water bottle my fingers gripped in heat so extreme
each knuckle swelled, my breath grew slow, my head pounded,

walking was difficult, thinking, how far can I make it
with nothing to pull along? I've nothing,
nothing behind me. No bottle turned toy,

no container empty enough to transform
into a caterpillar's sixteen bouncing legs,
waiting to grow the wings to support it in air.

In a matter of moments, I could shed my old skin,
pupating my greediness over what I did not offer,
though the boy did not consider me greedy. He waited

so patiently for me to hold the bottle to my lips
and drink the very last drop, having waited under rubble,
himself a survivor, overwintering in ash.

He sat next to me on the cracked cement steps,
leading to the collapsed second floor.
Water could not sustain him. He required nectar

sweet between leaves. It was all over the news.
The water was contaminated. Peacekeepers defecated in water,
bringing cholera to the Artibonite River.

The world's carelessness now set afloat.
I know. I was ready to discard my bottle,
set it on its journey of decomposition,

strip it of its corporeal form. My bottle,
held in the hands of so many people who will never
drink from it, those who delivered it from earth,

mined it, heated it, spun it a long while to become the axis
on which the day moves, wholly imaginary.
A boy waiting with a string in his hand.

Notes

"Ringaround Arosie": My inspiration for the use of the term DNA and for the poem "Up the Down Road," comes from my reading of Sandra Simonds' *Steal It Back*.

"Hang-Up" uses some language from the travel book *People of the Southwest*.

"My Oceanography" and "Chain Polymers": The expressions "A life-in-death feel," "deep is form," "was I some kind of man trap?" and "a vagina with teeth" appear in Eva Hesse's *Diaries*.

"Stone": *O the cry did knock against my very heart!* Shakespeare, *The Tempest*

"Eighter from Decatur": Lines 2–3 borrow some speech from Vaddey Ratner in *Music of the Ghosts*.

Many special thanks to Kate Sontag and to Cheryl Sucher, Marilyn Chin, and Jill Bialosky and to Dawn McDougall, Henry Israeli, Jeffrey Ethan Lee, Jo Pitkin, Michael Waters, Mihaela Moscaliuc, E. Ethelbert Miller, Baron Wormser, and to the irrepressible Colette Inez whose spirit, I am certain, hovers over these pages. Warmest appreciation for the crew at CavanKerry.

Acknowledgments

Grateful acknowledgment is given to the editors of the following publications in which some of these poems appeared, sometimes in a different form:

The Academy of American Poets, Poem-a-Day: "Axis Mundi"
Apiary: "Chain Polymers," "Just Before"
The Chiron Review: "Bumming a Cigarette"
Denver Quarterly Review: "Scylla and Charybdis"
Drunken Boat: "Flesh," "Jacket"
Ghost Town: "Ishtar," "Your Mind," "Your Words"
Great River Review: "Urban Myth"
Gulf Coast: "The Road Between the Rims"
Harvard Review: "Swimming in a Glass"
H_NGM_N: "Crush"
The Iowa Review: "Hang-Up"
Many Mountains Moving: "Alarm," "Cold," "Self-Study"
Per Contra: "Hunger"
Plume: "My Oceanography"
32 Poems: "In Service to a Bird"

CavanKerry's Mission

CavanKerry Press is committed to expanding the reach of poetry to a general readership by publishing poets whose works explore the emotional and psychological landscapes of everyday life.

Other Books in the Emerging Voices Series

The Singers I Prefer, Christian Barter
Momentum, Catherine Doty
An Imperfect Lover, Georgianna Orsini
Soft Box, Celia Bland
Rattle, Eloise Bruce
Eye Level: Fifty Histories, Christopher Matthews
GlOrious, Joan Cusack Handler
The Palace of Ashes, Sherry Fairchok
Silk Elegy, Sondra Gash
So Close, Peggy Penn
Kazimierz Square, Karen Chase
A Day This Lit, Howard Levy